The Jesus Comfort Quilt

A Coloring Book For Kids and Adults Grieving a Loss

This coloring book

is dedicated with great love

to my daughters, Lynn and Karen.

A publication of: Beyond the Blue Ministries, PO Box 498, Kingston, WA 98346
Beyond the Blue Ministries is a tax-exempt 501(c)(3) ministry.
© 2013 by Jane Van Antwerp. All rights reserved. Published 2013. Printed in Ann Arbor, MI.
16 15 14 13   1 2 3 4
ISBN (paperback): 978-1-939073-03-7
Books distributed to the trade by Seattle Book Company: www.SeattleBookCompany.com
Cover illustration by Jane Van Antwerp. Cover design by Sheila Cowley.

Dear Adult,

Children who have experienced a loss, whether from a death, divorce, illness, or even a disaster grieve. As adults, we cannot fix their grief, but we can be a significant help to them as they go through it.

This book was created by a Children's Pastor to help elementary-aged children and a caring adult to think and talk about both sadness and comfort. Conversations about serious topics are easier to enter when we are doing something alongside someone, rather than being face-to-face.

Our Lord Jesus wept when his close friend Lazarus died (John 11:33–36). In the Bible we see over and over again how important grieving is. However, kids cannot handle intense emotion for very long. They need to play and laugh and be loved in the midst of their grief. This is healthy.

Not all kids who receive this coloring book will gravitate to it. Nevertheless, we encourage you to give it to them and make it available. If you live with the child or teen, you can suggest coloring one quilt square together each night. There is no particular order, let them pick one that looks interesting to them. It may even become more helpful as the child grows older.

The last of the "quilt squares" is intentionally left blank so that children can talk about and draw what has brought comfort to them. God knows your child and the loss your child is experiencing so well; He will bring loving comfort over time in a very personal way. This is a promise to lean on and pray for (2 Corinthians 1:3–4).

Turn the page for ideas on making paper or cloth quilts.

To see all our resources, or to order more coloring books, visit us online at
www.beyondtheblueministries.com or mail a donation and your request to:
Beyond the Blue Ministries, PO Box 498, Kingston, WA 98346

Bulk discounts available for ministry purposes. Go to www.beyondtheblueministries.com

Beyond the Blue Ministries is a 501(c)(3) non-profit ministry. All gifts are tax deductible and greatly appreciated.

Instructions to Make a Jesus Comfort Quilt

The quilt squares found on each page can be cut out and made into a paper quilt, or transferred to be the squares for a cloth quilt. We encourage you to let the child pick out eight of the pages he or she likes or finds most helpful and use these to make a special "Jesus comforter." Use the first-page picture of Jesus as the ninth and center quilt square. Leave the half-inch border around the dotted lines so that each quilt square will be 8.5" x 8.5".

To make a paper quilt as a poster for your child's room, we suggest you use colored butcher paper or wrapping paper as the "backing" on which the quilt squares will be glued. It should be at least 27" x 27" to give a little border around and between each square. If you are making a cloth quilt, make it larger so that it can be a nice comforter for a bed or couch.

The act of creating a special project together can itself bring comfort.

Jesus said, "Blessed are those who mourn, for they will be comforted" (Matthew 5:4). Although hard to understand, it is good to know that even when awful things happen and we are sad, Jesus promises to bring us comfort. It doesn't come all at once—He knows it takes lots of time after a big loss, but little surprising things will help us and bring us small doses of comfort.

When we are sad, God often brings someone to say something kind to us. These words are true and helpful. It might surprise you who He brings! The person may even be younger than you! Keep a journal and write the kind words they share. Jesus also has kind words to say to you right now; you can hear them by reading Isaiah 43:1–4a.

Hearing Kind Words

When we are very sad, we feel and think a lot of things—things we may never have thought about before. That's okay. But it is really helpful to find an adult who can listen to those thoughts and help you. You are so important. And what you are going through is very hard. Remember that Jesus is also a good listener and always has the time for you.

Did you know that kids need to play? Jesus knows this. He loved playing when He was a kid. Adults can handle being serious longer than kids can. So when you need to play… DO! Maybe invite an adult to play with you. That adult just might need to laugh and enjoy being with you. It is good to be together when we are sad.

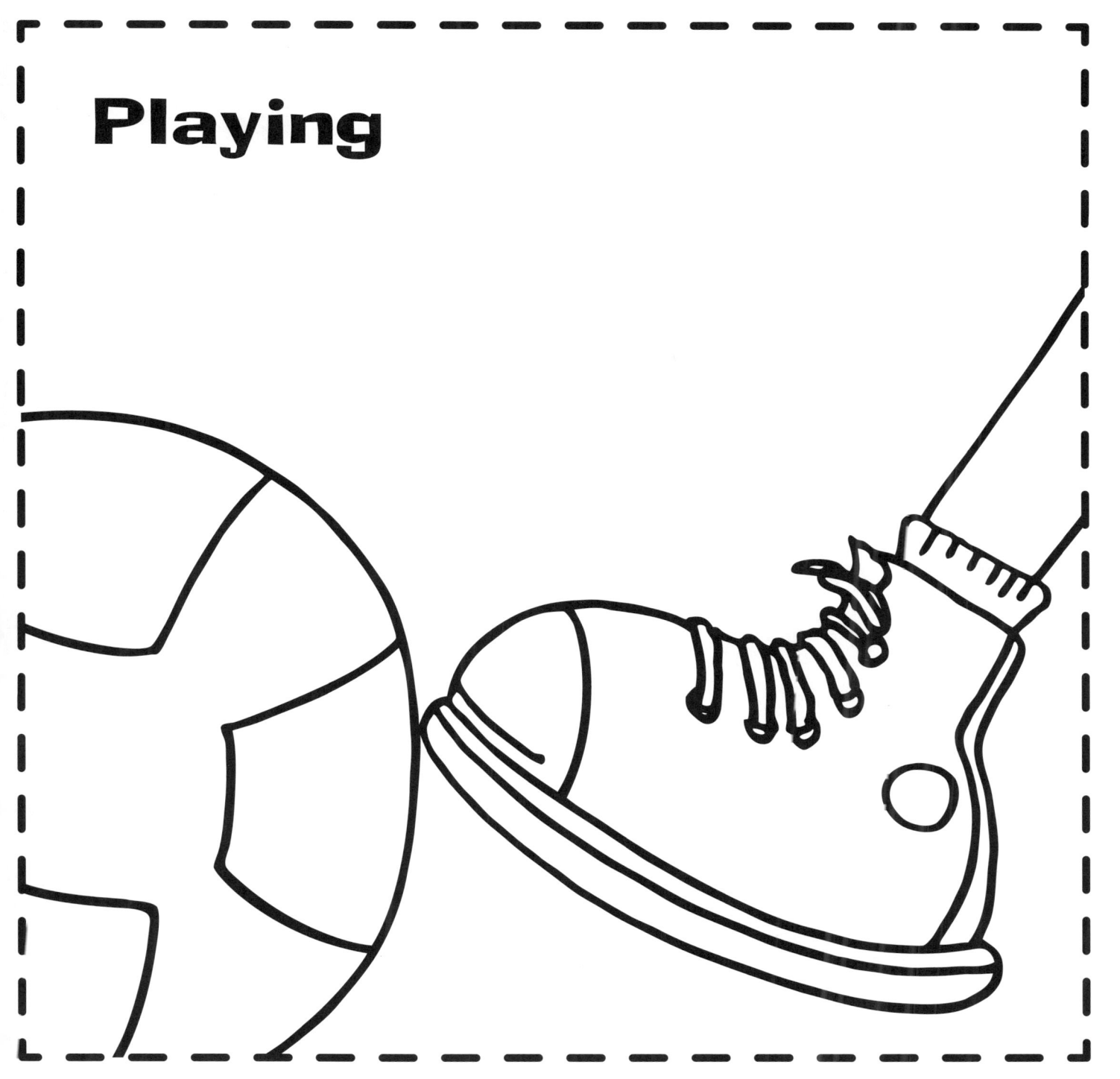

If other people know about the hard thing
that is happening to you, they may ask to hug you.
You can say "no" if you want to. But if you want
a hug from your family or friends, it is a quick
and wonderful reminder that they love you.
Do you need a hug?

A Hug

Many people love receiving a gift when they are hurting, even if it is very small. A gift can't fix our sadness, but it tells us that someone thought of us. Even though you are sad, it feels good to say "thank you" for every gift and card you receive.

A Gift

It's hard to sing when we are sad. But God gives us songs to help us say things and hear things and feel things. Do you have a favorite song about God? When you hear or sing it, does it help you?

A Song About God

Good stories are important. It is sometimes good to escape into another world. Sometimes a story tells us a truth that helps us when we are sad. Have you heard a story like that? There are a lot of stories in the Bible. Do you have a favorite?

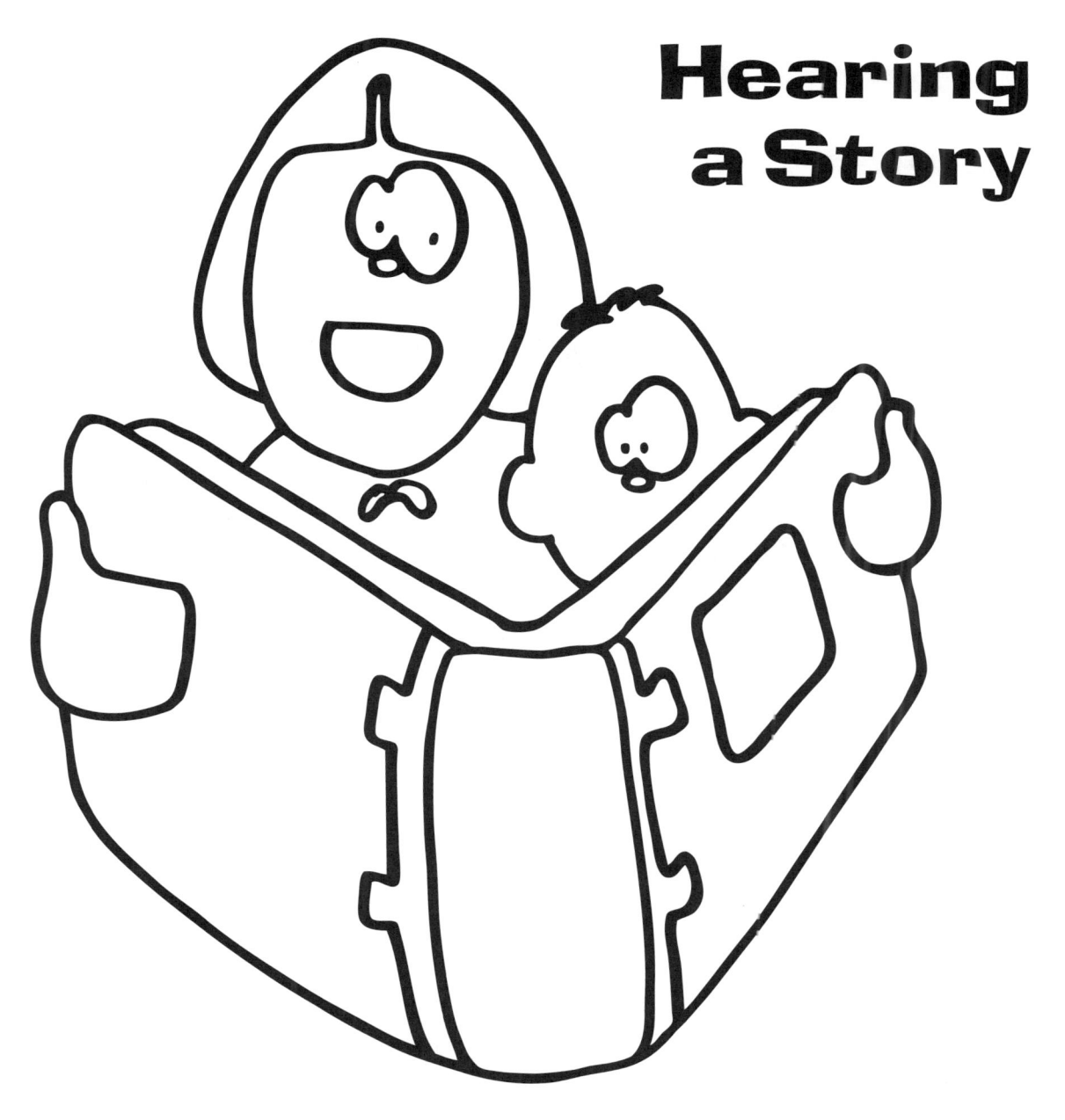

Besides you, who else is sad? Is there something you can do to help that person? How have things changed? Is there something new you can start to do to help your family? When you help, it brings comfort to you!

As we grow up, we sometimes think we are too big to be held. But in reality we all need to be held when we are sad. We feel more loved and secure when we are more than hugged, when we are held tight by someone safe and loving. Even when there is no one to hold you—God is holding you!

Being Held

Jesus always has a message for you. That message is exactly what you most need to hear. That message is usually a Bible verse or even a whole Bible story! Sometimes we find that message by reading the Bible ourselves; sometimes the Bible verse is written in a card, or spoken by a friend, or quoted in a sermon. Sometimes the Holy Spirit reminds you of a verse you have already memorized!

Reading a Bible Verse

When we have a big crisis, things change. Sometimes we long to do normal stuff and have everyone act the way they used to. Is this true for you? What do you most miss doing? Some day in the future, the changes that have happened and the new ways of doing things will feel normal. Ask God for help with this; He knows it is super hard.

Doing Normal Stuff

When someone we love dies, we feel incredibly sad. And even though it hurts, it is important to remember the good times you had with that person. You will never lose the best of the past, but life will not be the same from now on. It is important to remember. Maybe you want to make a memory keepsake box or a special photo album to help you remember.

Jesus loves to talk to us and to hear from us through prayer. He wants to hear how we hurt. In the Bible there are a lot of sad prayers, even prayers when people tell God how He seemed to have let them down. It is so important to keep talking to God and asking Him for help. He loves you and hurts when you hurt.
Read the prayer in Psalm 42:3–5.

The Bible tells us Jesus cried. People don't like to cry, but crying is very natural when we are sad. What we feel is very important, and our feelings sometimes come out in tears. So it is okay for you to cry when you need to. And if Jesus cried, it is okay if adults cry too. God sees every tear drop and loves us so.

Tears

Sometimes when we are very sad and we can only think of who and what we miss, it is hard to think of something we are thankful for. But when we do think of something and say thanks, it helps give us a little bit of comfort.

Sometimes a huge loss or crisis brings us a lot of questions and maybe even confusion. This is natural. We want to know why things happen. We want to understand. But we may never really understand while we live here on earth. This is so hard for us! Keep telling God all the things you are thinking about. He loves you and sees you and is big enough to trust. You can trust that He is working even when you can't see and don't fully understand.

Sometimes we think that since our lives
have changed, who we are has changed too.
God wants us to know that the most important
thing about who we are has not changed AND
will never change. You are God's loved child.
You matter so much to Him. He knows your
every thought, sees every tear, and
loves you no matter what.

Sometimes when we are sad, we don't want to go anywhere or see anybody. We might be afraid of what people will say, think that we will cry, or just want to be left alone. Eventually, though, it is important to worship and remember that God is even bigger than our sadness. God is even bigger than what has happened. When we are sad, being in the presence of God is the best way to find comfort.

Worshiping

When bad things happen, it is hard to think that things will ever be better. That is because we are hurting. But because of Jesus, we can have hope. Jesus died on the cross to forgive us. This is so good, but Jesus didn't stop there! He didn't stay dead. He came back to life on Easter morning. So even when awful things happen, we know Jesus has hope for us. Our hope is Heaven and living with Him forever.

What brings you comfort?
What helps even just a little bit?
What helps you feel more loved,
less alone, stronger, more hopeful?
Draw a picture, or write the
words in this box.